WORDS TO HELP YOU

BE A
SUCCESS

Other Titles in This Series:

*Words to Help You Be Happy
in All the Ways That Matter Most*

*Words to Help You
Be Positive Every Day*

*Words to Help You Be Strong
Along the Path of Life*

We wish to thank Susan Polis Schutz for permission to reprint the following poems that appear in this publication: "When you follow your passion…" and "People Who Achieve Success." Copyright © 1986, 2004 by Stephen Schutz and Susan Polis Schutz. And for "This life is yours…." Copyright © 1979 by Continental Publications. All rights reserved.

Library of Congress Control Number: 2008928040
ISBN: 978-1-59842-253-5

⋔ and Blue Mountain Press are registered in U.S. Patent and Trademark Office.
Certain trademarks are used under license.

Acknowledgments appear on page 72.

Printed in China.
First Printing: 2008

♻ This book is printed on recycled paper.

This book is printed on fine quality, laid embossed, 80 lb. paper. This paper has been specially produced to be acid free (neutral pH) and contains no groundwood or unbleached pulp. It conforms with the requirements of the American National Standards Institute, Inc., so as to ensure that this book will last and be enjoyed by future generations

Blue Mountain Arts, Inc.
P.O. Box 4549, Boulder, Colorado 80306

Words to Help You

Be a

Success

Edited by Kate McIntyre

Blue Mountain Press™

Boulder, Colorado

*S*uccess is thinking big, aiming high, and shooting far. It's taking a dream and doing anything, risking everything, and stopping at nothing to make it a reality.

— *Caroline Kent*

Introduction

*W*ise words are such wonderful things. Just a few perfect words, spoken or shared at the right time, can change our lives. They can keep us healthy and safe and strong. They can guide us and inspire us. They can teach us how to travel life's path in the best possible way... and avoid some of the problems and pitfalls. They can give us courage. They can give us faith.

Within the pages of this book, you will discover some of the most encouraging and insightful advice you've ever heard. You will be introduced to a number of things you've never read before — but that you'll never forget for as long as you live.

These pearls of wisdom come from a wide variety of remarkable people who share a common message. They believe in being successful, in choosing wisely, and in making each day as rewarding as it can possibly be.

Listen to their conversation, take their messages to heart, and let their words help you be a success... as you continue on your journey through life.

— *Douglas Pagels*

You Are Destined
to Be a Success

*D*on't ever forget that you are unique.
Be your best self
and not an imitation of someone else.
Find your strengths
and use them in a positive way.
Don't listen to those
who ridicule the choices you make.
Travel the road that you have chosen
and don't look back with regret.
You have to take chances
to make your dreams happen.
Remember that there is plenty of time
to travel another road —
    and still another —
in your journey through life.
Take the time to find the route
that is right for you.

— *Jacqueline Schiff*

The First Step Is Knowing Who You Are...

I now understand that true power has very little to do with what's on your résumé. It's about being true to yourself and finding your own voice and path in the world. The way you come to your power is through your life's experiences and knowing who you are.

— *Maria Shriver*

*A*s the old saying goes, you better know what you want because you might get it and you've got to accept it. Whether you succeed or whether you encounter adversity, you always have to believe in your worth as a person. That's what counts.

— *Author Unknown*

...and Where You Want to Go

All of us have a built-in compass to help us get to wherever we desire to go. Don't forget to trust that compass, and refer to it often, for with that trusting will come the strength to bear whatever life deals you.

— *Donna Fargo*

I will not follow where the path may lead, but I will go where there is no path, and I will leave a trail.

— *Muriel Strode*

Believe in Yourself

You know that voice somewhere inside you that says you can do anything? Listen to it. That voice is your heart, your passion, your destiny speaking, and it knows what it's talking about. Let it pull you toward your dreams.

And if you ever start to hear a voice that says you can't do it, just remember *that* voice is always wrong.

Believe in yourself. You are destined for great things.

— *Alyssa Rienne*

*H*e who is bound to a star
does not turn back.

— *Leonardo da Vinci*

*I*f you have built castles in the air, your work need not be lost; that is where they should be. Now put the foundations under them.

— *Henry David Thoreau*

*T*he greater danger for most of us is not that our aim is too high and we miss it, but that it is too low and we reach it.

— *Michelangelo*

*F*ar away there in the sunshine are my highest aspirations. I may not reach them, but I can look up and see their beauty, believe in them, and try to follow where they lead.

— *Louisa May Alcott*

$\mathcal{I}$'m big on aspiration mainly because I don't fully believe in lucky breaks, fairy godmothers, or men on white horses coming to save the day. I think you have to want things for yourself, make them happen for yourself, and take risks to put your own dreams into motion. Once you do that, it's amazing how the doors start opening — but they don't swing wide when you're hanging out at home reading your old *Cosmo* magazines for the fourth time in a row. Don't get me wrong: I'm not saying you should simply aspire to make a ton of cash or get famous. Instead, I think that first and foremost, you should aspire to a level of personal excellence — to be the best you can be.

— Kimora Lee Simmons

Discover Your Life's Passion...

*E*nthusiasm is one of the most powerful engines of success. When you do a thing, do it with all your might.... Be active, be energetic, be enthusiastic and faithful, and you will accomplish your objective.

— *Ralph Waldo Emerson*

I think I overcame every single one of my personal shortcomings by the sheer passion I brought to my work. I don't know if you're born with this kind of passion, or if you can learn it. But I do know you need it. If you love your work, you'll be out there every day trying to do it the best you possibly can, and pretty soon everybody around will catch the passion from you — like a fever.

— *Sam Walton*

...and Let It Carry You Toward Your Goals

When you follow your passion, you want to do the best job you can and your chance of success increases. Pursuing what you like to do is a "success" in itself.

— *Susan Polis Schutz*

$\mathcal{F}$ollow your hopes and dreams while you can. While the desire is burning. When the chance comes your way. Don't be a ship that stays in the harbor, never straying from its safety. Don't get tangled up with "maybe... maybe someday." Too many folks will tell you that if you spend your whole life waiting, "someday" arrives too little, too late.

Maybe it's already a little later than it seems. If you really want to do it, do it while you can. Be brave... and sail away on your dreams.

— Douglas Pagels

$\mathcal{I}$ don't know if I can have it all,
but I do know that I want it all.

— Madonna

$\mathcal{R}$elinquish your attachment to the known, step into the unknown, and you will step into the field of all possibilities. In your willingness to step into the unknown, you will have the wisdom of uncertainty factored in. This means that in every moment of your life, you will have excitement, adventure, mystery. You will experience the fun of life — the magic, the celebration, the exhilaration, and the exultation of your own spirit.

— *Deepak Chopra*

$\mathcal{T}$he men who try to do something and fail are infinitely better than those who try to do nothing and succeed.

— *Lloyd Jones*

Take a Chance...

*T*he important thing is this:
to be able at any
moment to sacrifice
what we are
for what we could become.

— *Charles du Bois*

...Just Go for It

I come across so many people in all walks of life who have the urge to try something new, but simply can't pull the trigger to do it.... The biggest reason I find people don't take risks is that, well, they're comfortable where they are. That may make you feel safe but it won't allow you to grow.

— *Jerry Rice*

*K*atharine Hepburn once told me, "It's not what you do in life, it's what you finish!" But many people don't even start, because they are afraid of failure. To me the only failure is when you don't even try. So set your path, be brave, do your best and *smile*, because you are doing all of the above.

— *Martina Navratilova*

Expect the Best...

Successful, happy people continually
maintain an attitude of positive
self-expectancy. They expect to be
successful in advance, and they are
seldom disappointed. They expect
to make more sales than they lose.
They expect to learn something
valuable from every experience. They
expect to eventually achieve their goals,
and they remain open to the possibility
that those goals may be achieved in a
way that they didn't expect.

...*So Often, You'll Achieve It*

The very best way to predict the future
is to *create* it, and you create your future
by the way you approach everything that
happens to you today, either positively
or negatively. If you approach each
situation confidently expecting to learn
from it or gain from it, you will continue
to grow and progress and move toward
your goals. You will also be a happier,
more optimistic person that other people
will want to be around and to help.

— *Brian Tracy*

Success Is What Happens When You Don't Give Up

*Y*our dreams are
just around the corner —
waiting to come true.
Believe in yourself
and know your hard work,
persistence, and dedication
    will pay off.
And when they do...
they will be extra sweet
because you will know
you have earned your rewards.
May you achieve
all that you wish for — and more.

— *Jason Blume*

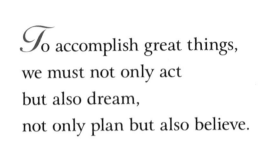

*T*o accomplish great things,
we must not only act
but also dream,
not only plan but also believe.

— *Anatole France*

The Habit of Success

What you do consistently and repeatedly grows stronger. And that provides you with nearly unlimited opportunity.

Success is not a secret that is hidden from you. Success is a habit that is readily available to you.

Life is made up of moment after moment. Point all those moments in the same direction, and truly magnificent achievements will come about.

There are very few things of value that you can create instantly. Yet when you expand your horizon to a few weeks or months, the possibilities for achievement increase dramatically.

The hours and the days will pass whether you make use of them or not. Choose to focus your energy in a specific direction, again and again, and put the power of time to work for you.

Keep your thoughts, your words and your actions pointed in the direction you would most like to go. Develop the habit of success, and with it you can create whatever you choose.

— *Ralph Marston*

Stay Focused

You can have anything you want — if you want it badly enough. You can be anything you want to be, have anything you desire, accomplish anything you set out to accomplish — if you will hold to that desire with singleness of purpose.

— *Robert Collier*

$\mathcal{T}$he power of disciplined focus is the secret of success. To focus means to bring your attention to the center, to concentrate on one thing intently in order to gain clarity. Teaching yourself to stay focused on one project, goal, or opportunity at a time will not only allow you to be more productive and effective, it can also challenge you to go more deeply into the task at hand and bring forth more creative insight and wisdom.

Too often we try to "cover all the bases," respond to every opportunity, or provide every possible service that someone might need, in the hopes of striking success. But the truth is, long-term, sustainable success often comes from the ability to stay focused on one project or goal at a time.

— *Cheryl Richardson*

One Secret All Successful People Know...

*O*ne of the great lessons I've learned… is that you've got to discipline your life. No matter how good you may be, you've got to be willing to cut out of your life those things that keep you from going to the top.

— *Bob Richards*

*T*he difference between someone who is successful and someone who isn't is not about talent. It's about preparation. So much of what successful people do — knowing the competition, making their luck, being equipped to take risks, overcoming adversity, dealing with success — is tied to the powerful principle of preparation.

— *Mike Shanahan*

...Hard Work Is the Quickest Route to Your Goals

*Y*ou have to be willing to put the work in that's required. I know a couple of people who've been successful by accident, but they usually don't stay successful by accident. Then they have to put the work in.... You've got to make a decision in your life that it is going to take a certain amount of work to get to this place and then maintain that place. And if you're not willing to do the amount of work, then you should settle for something less.

— *Matt Lauer*

I have been underqualified for every job I've ever had. But wherever I went, I worked harder than the next guy. If you're humble and hardworking, opportunities will arise for you.

— *Rachel Ray*

$\mathcal{D}$o not scatter your powers. Engage in one kind of business only, and stick to it faithfully until you succeed, or until you conclude to abandon it. A constant hammering on one nail, will generally drive it home at last, so that it can be clinched. When a man's undivided attention is centered on one object, his mind will constantly be suggesting improvements of value, which would escape him if his brain were occupied by a dozen different subjects at once. Many a fortune has slipped through men's fingers by engaging in too many occupations at once.

— *P. T. Barnum*

$\mathcal{Y}$our own resolution to succeed is more important than any other one thing.

— *Abraham Lincoln*

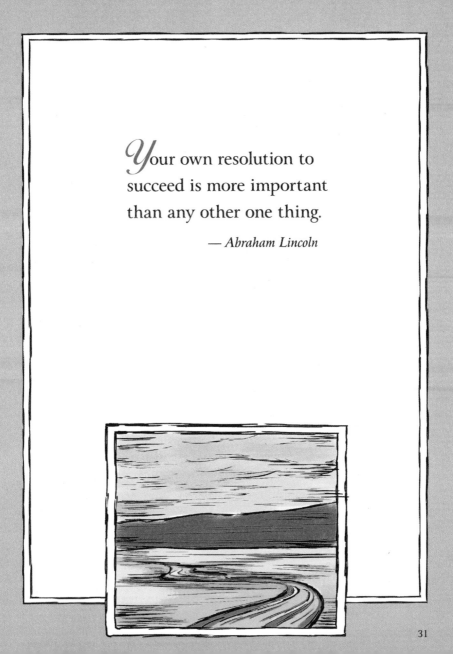

There are two primary reasons for setting goals. First, they give you focus. Second, they give you direction.

Focus. Without focus, it is difficult to hit a bull's-eye, take a good picture, or avoid getting killed on a busy highway. Focus is an essential ingredient in successful people. They keep their eye on the ball. Yes, there are distractions, unexpected circumstances, and unknowns that will have an impact on you keeping your focus; but you must focus if you want to succeed.

Direction. The ultimate achievement of a goal is less important than the ability to continue working toward it. Many people achieve their goals and are disappointed once they get them. A goal once achieved is a milestone, yes, but you can't just sit back and rest on your success.

When a winner doesn't reach a goal, he or she reexamines what needs to change and then changes the time frame to achieve it. When a loser doesn't reach a goal, he or she reexamines and then changes the goal.

Don't worry about the destination; keep your eye on the ball in the present with what you can do now, not tomorrow. Do something every day to move a little closer to your objective.

— *Tim Connor*

If Success Is Your Goal...

Become a planner. Examine every project in detail before you commit to it and plan every step you will have to take to make it succeed. Try to limit the surprises that will arise as the project proceeds. Don't dismiss any potential problem as too minor or unlikely.

— *Donald Trump*

...Planning Is Your Key

*E*stablishing goals is critical. Goals are the detailed road maps to your dreams. If you don't have goals providing the direction, how in the world are you going to find your way there?

— *Mike Shanahan*

*D*on't lose the forest for the trees. Don't spend all your time doing the urgent but short-term tasks; take time to do the strategic planning. If you are running really hard, but in the wrong direction, you're just wasting time.

— *Dr. Mehmet Oz*

Find a Mentor...

I would not have had the success I've had without several people's wisdom and knowledge to get me out of sticky situations. I believe everyone needs some kind of proximity to a mentor, an advisor, or maybe a whole handful of people who can keep nudging you along the way.... You'd be surprised how many people are flattered to be asked for advice and insight.

— *Kimora Lee Simmons*

*N*o one in this life gets ahead without the help of a lot of other people. Even the most talented need others to point out the way or lend a hand.

— *Tavis Smiley*

...Who Will Help You Succeed

*T*here is a wonderful way to cut twenty years off the learning curve in your career. It is to hang out with people who are where you want to be, or people who have done what you want to do.... A mentor is one of many ways to accomplish this objective.

— *Tim Connor*

*B*e on the lookout for good coaches. Watch their lives, listen to their advice... and believe them. You may never achieve what you want to accomplish if you don't have someone in your life who has already found what you are striving for.

— *Orel Hershiser*

$\mathscr{T}$he fellow asked the bearded sage he met on the path, "Which way is success?" The monk said nothing and gestured down the path. The seeker was elated by the prospect that success was so close and so easy, and rushed ahead.

Suddenly, there comes the sound of *splat*. In a little while, the seeker, now tattered and stunned, limps back, assuming he must have taken a wrong turn. He repeats his question to the guru, who again points silently in the same direction. The seeker nods, turns, and heads back in the same direction as before. This time, the sound of *splat* is deafening. When the seeker crawls back, he is bloody, broken, and angry. Screaming at the monk, he demands to know why he was sent off in the direction of disaster. "No more pointing. Talk!"

Only then does the guru speak. "Success is that way," he said. "Just a little past splat."

— *Jerry Porras, Stewart Emery,*
and Mark Thompson

$\mathcal{W}$e learn wisdom from failure much more than from success. We often discover what will do by finding out what will not do; and probably he who never made a mistake never made a discovery.

— *Samuel Smiles*

Failure Is No Fun...

Failure is a reality; we all fail at times and it's painful when we do. But it's better to fail while striving for something wonderful, challenging, adventurous, and uncertain than to say, "I don't want to try, because I may not succeed completely."

— *Jimmy Carter*

Failure is the condiment that gives success its flavor.

— *Truman Capote*

...but It Can Be a Great Teacher

You're going to lose more than you're going to win, no matter who you are. Most of us overreact when we lose, and over-celebrate when we win, and I'm no exception. I have a love-hate relationship with losing: it makes me brooding and quarrelsome. But the fact is, a loss is its own inevitable lesson, and it can be just as valuable as a victory in the range of experiences, if you'll examine it.

— *Lance Armstrong*

Courage Gets You Through the Hard Times...

*A*bolish fear and you can accomplish whatever you wish.

— Elbert Hubbard

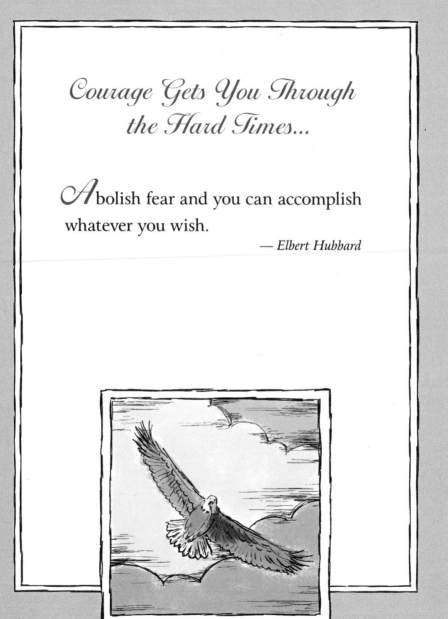

...the Key Is to Believe in Yourself

*Y*ou gain strength, courage, and confidence by every experience in which you really stop to look fear in the face.

You are able to say to yourself, "I lived through this horror. I can take the next thing that comes along."

The danger lies in refusing to face the fear, in not daring to come to grips with it. If you fail anywhere along the line it will take away your confidence. You must make yourself succeed every time. *You must do the thing you think you cannot do.*

— *Eleanor Roosevelt*

The Race for Success Is Not a Sprint...

The difference between a successful man and others is not in the lack of strength, nor in the lack of knowledge, but rather in the lack of will.

— *Vince Lombardi*

One can go a long way after one is tired.

— *French proverb*

...It's a Marathon

*L*ove what you do. Believe in your instincts. And you'd better be able to pick yourself up and brush yourself off every day. While life is not always fair, it is manageable. It is a matter of attitude and confidence.

— *Mario Andretti*

*C*onsider the postage stamp. It secures success through its ability to stick to one thing until it gets there.

— *Josh Billings*

Take the Power...

$\mathcal{T}$his life is yours
Take the power
to choose what you want to do
and do it well
Take the power
to love what you want in life
and love it honestly
Take the power
to walk in the forest
and be a part of nature

...to Make Your Life a Success

Take the power
to control your own life
No one else can do this for you
Nothing is too good for you
You deserve the best
Take the power
to make your life
healthy
exciting and worthwhile
The time is now
Take the power
to create a successful
happy
life

— *Susan Polis Schutz*

Only You Can Decide...

The great pleasure in life is doing
what people say you cannot do.

— *Walter Bagehot*

Success is not measured
by how well you fulfill
the expectations of others,
but by how honestly
you live up to
your own expectations.

— *Linda Principe*

...*What Success Means in Your Life*

*L*et the world know you as you are,
not as you think you should be, because
sooner or later, if you are posing, you will
forget the pose, and then where are you?

— *Fanny Brice*

*M*any people say I'm the best
women's soccer player in the world.
I don't think so. And because of
that, someday I just might be.

— *Mia Hamm*

$\mathcal{S}$uccess means something different
    to each one of us,
but it comes to those
    who are willing to work hard
and who continue to be dedicated
    to making their dreams come true.

Success means setting goals
and focusing yourself
in the right direction
    in order to reach them.
It means believing in yourself
    and constantly reminding yourself
that you are capable of achieving
    your desires.

Most of all,
success is being who you are,
and feeling proud of yourself
     for every task and challenge
that you face and conquer
     along the way.

— *Dena DiIaconi*

Don't Let Others Measure Your Achievements...

I don't know the key to success, but the key to failure is trying to please everybody.

— *Bill Cosby*

A man who trims himself to suit everybody will soon whittle himself away.

— *Author Unknown*

N othing would be done at all, if a man waited till he could do it so well, that no one could find fault with it.

— *Cardinal John Henry Newman*

...Real Success Comes from Within

*P*icture in your mind the able, earnest, useful person you desire to be, and the thought that you hold is hourly transforming you into that particular individual you so admire.

— *Elbert Hubbard*

*W*hether your dream is dollars or satisfaction, sainthood or popularity, fame or authenticity, what makes your dream worthy and real is that it is yours. You alone set the standard of what it means for you to succeed in life, for it is you alone who knows what will truly fulfill you in your heart and make your life worth living.

— *Chérie Carter-Scott, PhD*

*W*hen you have a winning attitude, negativity cannot influence your outlook on the future. Even in the aftermath of setbacks and disappointment your confidence quickly regains its stride, because you're so determined to make progress every day. You're comfortable taking paths that may lead you away from the crowd, because you measure success by no one's standards but your own.

— *Jon Peyton*

If you are true to yourself
in all that you do,
and if you keep working
to make your dreams
   come true...
then you will achieve success
just by doing your best.

You've got everything it takes
to be true to you.

— Ashley Rice

*A*lthough success can easily be defined as the achievement of goals, there's a difference between temporary and lasting success. I don't think you achieve lasting success unless you add another ingredient to the mixture, and that is to serve a cause greater than yourself. That's what lasting success is all about.

— *Senator John McCain*

*T*o excel is to reach your own highest dream. But you must also help others, where and when you can, to reach theirs. Personal gain is empty if you do not feel you have positively touched another's life.

— *Barbara Walters*

$\mathcal{S}$uccess, like happiness, cannot be pursued; it must ensue, and it only does so as the unintended side-effect of one's dedication to a cause greater than oneself or as the by-product of one's surrender to a person other than oneself. Happiness must happen, and the same holds for success: you have to let it happen by not caring about it.

— *Viktor E. Frankl*

$\mathcal{A}$ll success consists in this: You are doing something for somebody — benefiting humanity — and the feeling of success comes from the consciousness of this.

— *Elbert Hubbard*

*G*reatness is not found in possessions, power, position, or prestige. It is discovered in goodness, humility, service, and character.

— *William Ward*

Definition of a Successful Life

To laugh often and much;
to win the respect of intelligent people
and the affection of children;
to earn the appreciation of honest critics
and endure the betrayal of false friends;
to appreciate beauty, to find the best in others;
to leave the world a bit better,
whether by a healthy child,
a garden patch or a redeemed social condition;
to know even one life has breathed easier
because you have lived.

— *Ralph Waldo Emerson*

What Sets Winners Apart

Winners take chances. Like everyone else, they fear failing, but they refuse to let fear control them.

Winners don't give up. When life gets rough, they hang in until the going gets better.

Winners are flexible. They realize there is more than one way and are willing to try others.

Winners know they are not perfect. They respect their weaknesses while making the most of their strengths.

Winners fall, but they don't stay down. They stubbornly refuse to let a fall keep them from climbing.

Winners don't blame fate for their failures nor luck for their successes. They accept responsibility for their lives.

Winners are positive thinkers who see good in all things. From the ordinary, they make the extraordinary.

Winners believe in the path they have chosen. Even when it's hard, even when others can't see where they are going, winners are patient. They know a goal is only as worthy as the effort that's required to achieve it. And they make this world a better place to be.

— *Nancye Sims*

Success Means Loving Your Work, Family, Life...

When we look back on our lives from our deathbeds — a year from now, five years, ten, twenty, fifty, or whatever — it's almost certain that the most important aspects will not have been our ability to dominate others, collect achievements, win contests, and beat out our competition.

Instead, the things that will seem most important will be the quality of our lives. We will measure the success of our lives by the type of relationships we had with ourselves and with others. We will reflect upon our children, spouse or girlfriend, relatives, friends, colleagues, and other important people in our lives.

— *Richard Carlson*

...and Most Importantly, Loving Yourself!

*E*very day is an opportunity
to make the most...
of the <u>wonderful</u> person you are.

— *Collin McCarty*

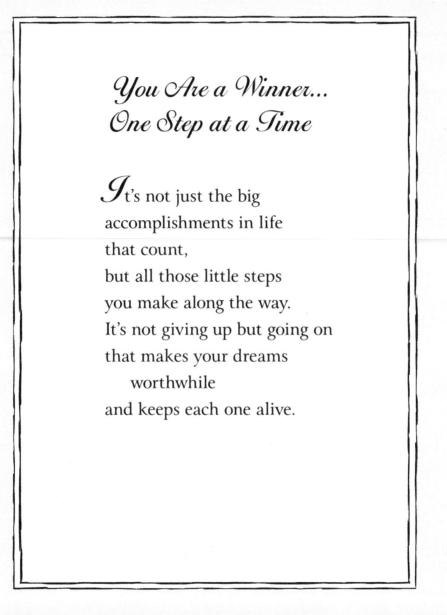

You Are a Winner...
One Step at a Time

It's not just the big
accomplishments in life
that count,
but all those little steps
you make along the way.
It's not giving up but going on
that makes your dreams
    worthwhile
and keeps each one alive.

In measuring your moments
    of success,
remember the history
behind each one.
Remember how your
determination
    to never quit
was the force behind
each accomplishment
and the guiding light
of every dream you achieved.
Never forget
that anything you want
can come true —
as long as you take it
one step at a time.

— Barbara J. Hall

People Who Achieve Success

They have confidence in themselves
They have a very strong sense of purpose
They never have excuses for not doing something
They always try their hardest for perfection
They never consider the idea of failing
They work extremely hard toward their goals
They know who they are
They understand their weaknesses
   as well as their strong points
They can accept and benefit from criticism
They know when to defend what they are doing
They are creative
They are not afraid to be a little different
   in finding innovative solutions that will
       enable them to achieve their dreams

— *Susan Polis Schutz*

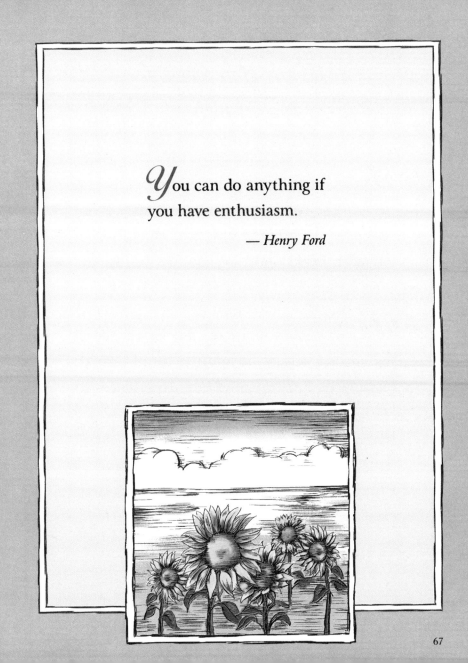

*𝒴*ou can do anything if
you have enthusiasm.

— *Henry Ford*

When You Reach the Summit...

$\mathcal{T}$here are two things to aim at in life: first, to get what you want; and, after that, to enjoy it. Only the wisest of mankind achieve the second.

— *Logan Pearsall Smith*

$\mathcal{F}$or as long as you are on this Earth, there will always be new adventures to take, new mountains to climb, and new experiences to learn from.... What matters along the way is that you pause every now and then to take stock of what you have accomplished and who you are before you set off on your next exciting journey.

— *Chérie Carter-Scott, PhD*

...Remember to Stop and Enjoy the View

Share your successes
   with the world.
Inspire others
   to reach for their own stars.

Let your achievements
stand as a shining example
that goals can be attained,
   fears can be conquered,
and dreams really can come true —
when we have the courage
   to pursue them.

— Jason Blume

You Are So Deserving
of Your Success

May your accomplishments cause you to reflect on what a gift your life is to yourself and others. The competition in the world is so great today, so every goal reached is something to be proud of. When all the elements come together to acknowledge someone's progress, it is truly something to celebrate.

May you be inspired to continue doing the things that are important to you and keep on making your dreams come true. May the pride others have in you encourage you to continue to pursue your purpose.

May your tomorrows hold new beginnings for you, and may your future be bright. May the joy of every lesson learned and every goal reached advance your feeling of fulfillment and keep you on a positive path.

— *Donna Fargo*

ACKNOWLEDGMENTS

We gratefully acknowledge the permission granted by the following authors, publishers, and authors' representatives to reprint poems or excerpts from their publications.

Caroline Kent for "Success is thinking big...." Copyright © 2008 by Caroline Kent. All rights reserved.

PARS International Corp for "I now understand that true power..." from "An Authentic Life" by Maria Shriver (*Newsweek*: October 15, 2007). Copyright © 2007 by Maria Shriver. All rights reserved.

Random House, Inc., for "Failure is the condiment..." from THE DOGS BARK by Truman Capote. Copyright © 1957, 1965, 1966, 1968, 1969, 1971, 1972, 1973 by Truman Capote. All rights reserved.

PrimaDonna Entertainment Corp. for "All of us have a built-in compass..." and "You Are So Deserving of Your Success" by Donna Fargo. Copyright © 1996, 2005 by PrimaDonna Entertainment Corp. All rights reserved.

ReganBooks, an imprint of HarperCollins Publishers, for "I'm big on aspiration..." and "I would not have had the success..." from FABULOSITY by Kimora Lee Simmons. Copyright © 2006 by Kimora Lee Simmons. All rights reserved.

Doubleday, a division of Random House, Inc., for "I think I overcame every single..." from SAM WALTON: MADE IN AMERICA by Sam Walton. Copyright © 1992 by the Estate of Samuel Moore Walton. All rights reserved. And for "It's a lesson I'll never forget" from WHAT I KNOW FOR SURE by Tavis Smiley with David Ritz. Copyright © 2006 by Tavis Smiley. All rights reserved.

Simon & Schuster Adult Publishing Group for "I don't know if I can have it all..." by Madonna from MADONNA: AN INTIMATE BIOGRAPHY by J. Randy Taraborrelli. Copyright © 2001 by J. Randy Taraborrelli. All rights reserved.

New World Library, Novato, CA, www.newworldlibrary.com, for "Relinquish your attachment to the known..." from SEVEN SPIRITUAL LAWS OF SUCCESS by Deepak Chopra. Copyright © 1994 by Deepak Chopra. All rights reserved.

Ballantine Books, a division of Random House, Inc., for "I come across so many people..." from GO LONG! by Jerry Rice with Brian Curtis. Copyright © 2007 by Jerry Rice. All rights reserved.

Lorne A. Adrain for "Katharine Hepburn once told me..." by Martina Navratilova, "Love what you do" by Mario Andretti, and "To excel is to reach your own..." by Barbara Walters from THE MOST IMPORTANT THINGS I KNOW, compiled by Lorne A. Adrain. Copyright © 1997 by Lorne A. Adrain. All rights reserved.

John Wiley and Sons, Inc., for "Successful, happy people continually maintain..." from CHANGE YOUR THINKING, CHANGE YOUR LIFE: HOW TO UNLOCK YOUR FULL POTENTIAL FOR SUCCESS AND ACHIEVEMENT by Brian Tracy. Copyright © 2005 by Brian Tracy. All rights reserved. And for "Become a planner" from TRUMP 101: THE WAY TO SUCCESS by Donald Trump. Copyright © 2007 by Trump University. All rights reserved.

Jason Blume for "Success Is What Happens When You Don't Give Up" and "Share your successes with the world....." Copyright © 2007, 2008 by Jason Blume. All rights reserved.

Ralph Marston for "The Habit of Success." Originally published in *The Daily Motivator* at www.dailymotivator.com. Copyright © 2007 by Ralph S. Marston, Jr. All rights reserved.

Wilder Publications, Inc., for "You can have anything you want..." from THE BOOK OF LIFE by Robert Collier. Copyright © 2007 by Robert Collier. All rights reserved.

Broadway Books, a division of Random House, Inc., for "The power of disciplined focus..." from LIFE MAKEOVERS by Cheryl Richardson. Copyright © 2000 by Cheryl Richardson. All rights reserved. And for "How do you learn to cope..." from EVERY SECOND COUNTS by Lance Armstrong. Copyright © 2003 by Lance Armstrong. All rights reserved. And for "Whether your dream is dollars or..." and for "For as long as you are on this Earth..." from IF SUCCESS IS A GAME, HERE ARE THE RULES by Chérie Carter-Scott, PhD. Copyright © 2000 by Chérie Carter-Scott, PhD. All rights reserved.

MacFarland & Company, Inc., for "One of the great lessons..." by Bob Richards from AMERICAN MEN OF OLYMPIC TRACK AND FIELD by Don Holst and Marcia Popp. Copyright © 2005 by Don Holst and Marcia Popp. All rights reserved.

HarperBusiness, a division of HarperCollins Publishers, for "The difference between someone..." and "Establishing goals is critical" from THINK LIKE A CHAMPION by Mike Shanahan. Copyright © 1999 by Mike Shanahan. All rights reserved.

Collins, an imprint of HarperCollins Publishers, for "You have to be willing to put..." by Matt Lauer and "Don't lose the forest for the trees" by Dr. Mehmet Oz from GOT WHAT IT TAKES? by Bill Boggs. Copyright © 2007 by Bill Boggs. All rights reserved.

The Good Housekeeping Institute for "I have been underqualified for every job..." by Rachel Ray from "Rachel Ray's Recipe for Joy" by Joanne Kaufman (*Good Housekeeping*: August 2006). Copyright © 2006 by Joanne Kaufman. All rights reserved.

Tim Connor for "There are two primary reasons..." and "There is a wonderful way..." from THE BASICS OF SUCCESS. Copyright © 2005 by Tim Connor. All rights reserved.

Grand Central Publishing for "Be on the lookout for good coaches" from BETWEEN THE LINES: NINE PRINCIPLES TO LIVE BY by Orel Hershiser. Copyright © 2001 by Orel Leonard Hershiser IV. Reprinted by permission of Grand Central Publishing. All rights reserved.

Wharton School Publishing for "The fellow asked the bearded sage..." by Jerry Porras, Stewart Emery, and Mark Thompson and "Although success can easily..." by John McCain from SUCCESS BUILT TO LAST by Jerry Porras, Stewart Emery, and Mark Thompson. Copyright © 2007 by Pearson Education, Inc. All rights reserved.

Crown Books, a division of Random House, Inc., for "Failure is a reality..." from SOURCES OF STRENGTH by Jimmy Carter, published by Times Books, a division of Random House, Inc. Copyright © 1999 by Jimmy Carter. All rights reserved. Reprinted by permission of Random House, Inc.

HarperCollins Publishers for "You gain strength..." from YOU LEARN BY LIVING by Eleanor Roosevelt. Copyright © 1960 by Eleanor Roosevelt. All rights reserved.

McGraw-Hill for "The difference between a successful man..." from WHAT IT TAKES TO BE #1 by Vince Lombardi. Copyright © 2003 by Vince Lombardi. All rights reserved.

Harold Matson Company, Inc., for "Let the world know you..." by Fanny Brice from THE FABULOUS FANNY: THE STORY OF FANNY BRICE by Norman Katkov, published by Alfred A. Knopf. Copyright © 1952, 1953 by Alfred A. Knopf, Inc. All rights reserved.

Quill, an imprint of HarperCollins Publishers, for "Many people say..." from GO FOR THE GOAL by Mia Hamm. Copyright © 1999, 2000 by Mia Hamm. All rights reserved.

Dena Dilaconi for "Success means something different..." Copyright © 2008 by Dena Dilaconi. All rights reserved.

Pedigree Books, a division of Penguin Group (USA), Inc., for "I don't know the key..." by Bill Cosby from TAKE IT FROM ME by Michael Levine. Copyright © 1996 by Michael Levine. All rights reserved.

Beacon Press, Boston, for "Success, like happiness..." from MAN'S SEARCH FOR MEANING by Viktor E. Frankl. Copyright © 1959, 1962, 1984, 1992 by Viktor E. Frankl. All rights reserved.

Hyperion for "One of the most effective..." from DON'T SWEAT THE SMALL STUFF FOR MEN by Richard Carlson, PhD. Copyright © 2001 by Richard Carlson, PhD. Reprinted by permission. All rights reserved.

Barbara J. Hall for "You Are a Winner... One Step at a Time." Copyright © 2008 by Barbara J. Hall. All rights reserved.

A careful effort has been made to trace the ownership of selections used in this anthology in order to obtain permission to reprint copyrighted material and give proper credit to the copyright owners. If any error or omission has occurred, it is completely inadvertent, and we would like to make corrections in future editions provided that written notification is made to the publisher:

BLUE MOUNTAIN ARTS, INC., P.O. Box 4549, Boulder, Colorado 80306.